With Love

Kelly & Ricardo

The Sacred Trust is dedicated to

Evelyn Catherine

and all mothers who endure.

We would like to acknowledge the support of Chuck Morris and all the folks at ANACAPA By The Sea for offering us a place to continue *LifeWorks* and the family and relationship work we believe in.

PARENTING
Guidance and Guardianship of Children

Introduction

"The future of the world does not lie in the hands of children. It lies in the hands that hold the hands of children. We cannot hold the hands of children until we hold the hands and heal the hearts of our own childness."

Parenting may be the ultimate *Sacred Trust.* What we offer our children is never lost. It extends through community, planetary guardianship and our children's children. Parenting is the single most impactful adventure one can embark on.

The following pages contain suggestions and tools for surviving and enjoying the journey of parenting the children we have and the children we are. Everyone is born into this world with a birthright. Our birthright includes the right to:
- nurturing and gentle touch
- be taken care of and taught to care for ourselves
- maintain ownership of our body
- chose friends
- feel whatever we feel
- own property
- be given and modeled limits
- encouragement to risk without excess pressure
- information and answers to our questions
- honesty about what is happening to us and around us
- taught boundaries and have them respected

Besides this birthright, each of us is born with a job to do.

A baby's job is to express needs; a parent's job is to listen to babies. As babies, we enter this world totally dependent on the people around us for survival. For many reasons parents are not always able to fulfill their job, sometimes because *their* parents were unable to, as were *their* parents and so on! It's both difficult and scary to be depended upon as parents when we were not able to depend on our own care givers. Fortunately, as babies we were incredibly resilient and adaptable; we learned quickly about who or what we could or couldn't depend on and in response learned to deny dependency needs or depend on externals and with these survival tools we made it through the short run. Unfortunately, many of these survival tools out live their usefulness and become the addictive and self destructive activities of adolescence and adulthood. Thus, many of our adult dependency problems stem from not having our child dependency needs met.

Parenthood is a sacred community every person is invited to join. Some of us choose to parent by joining in the process of co-creation. Others of us parent through our careers or participating in activities. As teachers, therapists, coaches, care givers, missionaries, social workers, helping professionals, writers, community leaders, co-workers and friends we have the opportunity to fulfill the sacred job of parenting. We all have opportunities to offer parenting to friends, those in need and of course ourselves.

The position of parenting is not to be better than, greater than or more important than those we parent. Roles of parents and children are *egalitarian*. The roles are very different yet both are equally as valuable as the other. We are children *and* parents. Regardless of the particular role we are in at any time, we are precious and unique beings.

The main job of parenting is to notice, label and affirm feelings and to model emotional fluency. When we need parenting, we need to be with people who affirm us, notice who we are and nurture and care about us. Being with people who are emotionally fluent, able to express their thoughts and feelings in words and body language clearly will help us to do the same. With this we're able to know ourselves and share and depend on others without losing our sense of self.

Good parenting isn't done by talking or telling others how to be or what to do. The best parenting is done through modeling. Teaching and parenting by talking and telling is like trying to drive a car with its horn - you can honk all day long and never get out of the garage! Modeling self respect of regular physical activity, seat belt use, getting enough rest, and healthy eating; modeling the joy of a belly laugh, family picnics, a stroll in the park, visiting with friends, or reading a good book; modeling the strength to be vulnerable by crying when it hurts, expressing fears and doubts, sharing our shame and joy; modeling the integrity of noticing creation, recycling and limiting consumption, standing up against abuse, admitting errors, apologizing, giving to those less fortunate than ourselves - all give an empowering parenting message of healthy and sound living.

Behaviors witnessed are the ones most likely to be replicated by those around us. How often do we give the conflicting message of "do as I say, not as I do," telling children to be honest while making up 'excuses' to get out of commitments or calling in sick to work when we're not or saying 'Don't use drugs' while using alcohol, nicotine or other drugs? *Children will hear more clearly what is modeled than what is said.*

Many problems in our culture stem from faulty, abusive or unavailable parenting. Crime, drug use, environmental destruction, stem from the same absence of boundary sense and self cherishing producing the despair and isolation at the roots of our cultural ills.

A child raised without healthy limits modeled won't recognize limits in consumption, spending or using. When dependency needs are not met the *interdependence* of the person with others or our planet isn't recognized. Without self esteem one easily becomes self and other destructive. When a child's vulnerability isn't embraced and affirmed the child learns to fear and disdain vulnerability within and without. This sets up the failure of our culture to help vulnerable groups in meaningful ways, including infants, children, people with differences and special problems, the homeless, those who live in poverty, high crime areas, and on Reservations. We can't recognize, embrace and care for the vulnerable aspects of our environment. *We project our fear and disdain of our vulnerability into a not noticing or caring for the vulnerability of others.*

Abuse stems from the failures of caregivers. This failure may be a consequence of our view of children. Frequently children are seen as property, chattel, to be owned and to do with as we please. We view them as extensions of us, a way to achieve immortality or to fulfill our unfulfilled lives. We set them on a path of being like us or to do what we could not do; to live out our dreams not theirs. We use them as objects of our anger and frustration or objects of our affection and seductive needs. They exist to fix our loneliness and fill our void. We believe we must control, punish, discipline and mold our children when we really need to learn from them about our childness and see them as a miracle of the gift of life itself.

As Gibran said in <u>The Prophet</u>:

> *"Your children are not your children.*
> *They are the sons and the daughters of life's longing for itself.*
> *They come through you, but they are not from you,*
> *And though they are with you they belong not to you.*
>
> *You may give them your love but not your thoughts,*
> *For they have their own thoughts.*
> *You may house their bodies but not their souls,*
> *For their souls dwell in the house of tomorrow, which you cannot visit, not even in your dreams.*
> *You may strive to be like them, but seek not to make them like you.*
> *For life goes not backward nor tarries with yesterday."*

We cannot appreciate the miracle of our children until we embrace the miracle of our childness. In our process of living and growing we need to find the parenting we may not have received in childhood. We are told to 'self-parent' but we can't give what we never received - even to ourselves. We can begin to find parenting by being with people who are kind and caring, who offer gentle support and notice us. As we grow and let the nurturing from others in, we'll be able to nurture our own childness and offer genuine caring to others.

On our journey we need to seek the mothering and fathering we missed. A word of caution: *do not go out to find a mother or a father, you already have them! Rather, seek nurturing and care giving from several sources.*

Parenting has nothing to do with age or gender. We can find parenting from people of all ages and backgrounds. The difference between mothering and fathering is mothering comes from women and fathering comes from a men! If a man teaches you to change a tire, fix the garage roof or mend a bird's broken wing, it's fathering. If a woman teaches you to change a tire, fix the garage roof or mend a bird's broken wing, it's mothering.

We also believe in finding *grandparenting* which doesn't necessarily mean finding an older person but rather hanging around someone who is sage, experienced and open to loving us just the way we are. Someone who nurtures us on our path of being who we were meant to be is the *grandest* parent of all!

In the following C's of Parenting we hope you find some suggestions and thoughts to add to your repertoire of sharing with and caring for others. We wish you well on your journey of parenting - your children and your childness!

Thirty-Six Suggestions For Enjoying and Surviving the Journey of Parenting

Committed

Many of us never decided to became parents. We simply had children. Maybe we did it because it was the 'thing to do', or it happened to us. We need a license to drive, to own a dog or bicycle, and to fish, but all we need to be a parent is an urge! The commitment to be a parent includes a decision to learn, mostly about us, but also about our children and the world. Our parenting will be a lifelong venture for most of us, so we might as well settle into it and learn what we can. In learning about us, our own childhood, we learn the most about parenting. It's in childhood we learn whether parenthood is a playground or a prison. What was our childhood like? How much of it are we duplicating or reacting to in our own parenting? Discovering us, for and through our children is a part of the parenting journey, but our meaning must come from our own lives, not from the lives of our children. Part of the commitment of child raising is to learn about children, their developmental stages, physical needs, readiness for learning and how they learn. Each child has a different style, a different personality, a different learning pattern. Albert Einstein once said, "everyone's a genius, some are just less damaged than others." We need to find their strengths and flat spots, give them touch and affirm their curiosity. They need support, affirmation, dependency, safety, trust. All of which begin with our commitment. Commitment eliminates abandonment. It's a lifetime of availability and care openly offered and our joy at making this commitment openly displayed.

❖❖❖❖❖

Compliment through affirmations

In affirming, we provide the setting for growth and joy. It's important not to compliment by telling them untrue things. They'll see and feel the lie and end up having less trust when we do notice something true. If they look awful, it's important not to say, "you look very nice today." It's also important not to focus so much on what they are wearing or how they look, but try to notice who they are. Compliments reinforce the external. To affirm is to notice what is on the inside rather than the outside. So much of our culture already over emphasizes how children should dress, what labels to wear, how to look and which hair style to have. All of this is pressure and fear for children that they won't fit in and does not increase their sense of self esteem or well being. *Affirm what you cannot photograph.* This will reinforce their identity and positive sense of self. Rather than being proud of them for their successes, affirm the pride they have of themselves. Affirm how they interact with other people, the kindness they show or when they stand up for themselves. They can be affirmed into living their life for them and not us. Affirming is creating a firm foundation upon which our children can rest and risk.

❖❖❖❖❖
Challenge

Children flourish when stimulated and challenged intellectually, physically and emotionally. All too often, we try to fix their losses, resolve their crises immediately, not giving them the chance to work it out, or do the healing. We can challenge them to identify their feelings, solve their problems, prioritize their lives and build a community of friends. We teach our children to challenge themselves when we challenge ourselves. Medium challenges offer the best opportunity for building self esteem. Too easy and there is little sense of accomplishment. Too difficult and they feel like failures. Through us they learn challenge. Working with them in their challenges, whether it be a puzzle, a game, a building project or homework, gives them a sense of support and reduces the feeling of overwhelm when presented with challenge. Letting them help us with our challenges, home improvement projects, or resolving our problems can give them not just a sense of importance but the ability and readiness to meet adult challenges and to know everyone has them.

Family vacations can be done around challenging adventures, hiking, biking, climbing, camps with a theme, tennis, or space. The challenge being to learn something and enjoy. Challenges of learning can be shared and modeled by study, reading and discussing. An important challenge, and a gift we can give our children is to find settings and times where there are few challenges except perhaps the challenges we face with our children as parents.

Children need to learn about life's challenges around money, career, and intimacy in a realistic way. Talking about these challenges with hope and commitment sets a positive posture for their future. When our challenges in life become overwhelming we need to share the reality with children, but not the burden. We need to get help. Then when our children's challenges become overwhelming, we'll be more able to be there for them and help them find outside help and resources. Challenge needs to be balanced with hope, spirituality and acceptance. Challenge is what facilitates healthy change and movement in our lives. As parents, it's important to remember growing up is a challenge. Our noticing it can make it a more joyful challenge for our children.   Growing up is to gain adulthood without losing childhood - which is one of the greatest challenges.

❖❖❖❖❖
Congruent

C ongruence is modeling a posture towards life where our beliefs, feelings, words and actions match. Modeling the congruent, appropriate expression for feelings reduces the need of our children to act out feelings. Congruence means our tone, facial expressions, words and body match what we're saying and the situation. If we've just experienced a loss and we're grieving, but our children come up and we pretend to be happy and smiling, they receive a double message. When they experience a loss, they won't know what to do with it. As parents, we can help them notice the ways they are reacting and feeling and help them be connected to what's happening. Commonly children and adults disconnect the reactions from the events. Our dog runs away, we get yelled at by a friend, an important project we worked on gets lost or was done wrong, and all of a sudden we feel sad, down and not very energetic. We may lose the connection between what's going on in our life, and our feelings of dejection. It can make a big difference if someone comes up and says "Boy, given what's happened the last few days for you, I'd feel really dejected too." The sadness is about the loss, having it affirmed, hearing what it's connected to, gives us a chance to move on. We encourage and teach congruence by noticing and linking the reactions to the action.

Careful

Full of care. Our relationships thrive when we reflect care. To show our children we don't just care about them, but we care for them and will be careful with them, gives them security and the ability to self care. Caring includes not projecting our worries on them but letting them know what's happening and we'll take care of it. Careful involves learning parenting skills, speculating the impact of statements we make to them and considering the result of our actions before acting. As a parent, being careful with ourselves and with our adult relationships especially our spouse or partner is as important as being full of care with our children. Being careful with ourselves reflects we care about ourselves.

Being careful in our relationships and with ourselves lets our children feel safer knowing they are in caring hands. Care is reflected in the tone of our voice, the expression in our face, the warmth of our eyes. Being careful with the planet, all of life, what is on loan to us is the outpouring of self care coming from careful parenting.

❖❖❖❖❖
Cautious

In our parental caution, we'll recognize children are resilient, but can be damaged. We reflect about what we say and do to and for them, teaching caution and safety around drug use, sexuality, seat belts, automobiles, strangers and friends. The world can be scary. There are scary places, things and people, and the more cautious we are when we get in those situations, the better chance we have of not being traumatized or hurt. Parenthood is a balance of modeling and teaching caution and of modeling and teaching risk taking. Areas of caution include who we bring into our home and lives, building a child proof home, limiting dangerous activities. Modeling a life of self protection through the wisdom of our adulthood. Over-caution and over-protection creates anxiety and worry. Our constant admonishment of our children about not doing this, being careful with that, is a reflection of our own insecurity, but feels like distrust to our children. Balance, trust and guiding concern enables healthy lifestyle.

❖❖❖❖❖
Consistent - not predictable

B e consistent in trust, availability, consequences, follow through and support. When not being consistent, move towards leniency and positive surprise, not angry mood swings. Keep them guessing but don't create insecurity. Consistently affirm, model affection, and consistently take care of yourself. By caring for us, we teach loved ones to take care of themselves. One of the more traumatic family processes for children is inconsistent parental control. It is less important how much control we exert in their life as it is to be consistent. Excess control can become intrusiveness, absence of any control can reflect neglect or non-caring. Swinging back and forth between the two can produce severe anxiety and becomes crazy-making. As care givers, we may consistently make mistakes but we can also consistently apologize, make amends and notice the mistakes as well as the impact and feelings our mistakes engender. An amend is not just "I'm sorry," it is a change. We can consistently be available to our children, but not necessarily present. Availability is much more important than hovering a few feet over our children's lives. Consistency in relationship is important, but also consistency in geography, friends and school. Consistent rituals, traditions and patterns have an impact on a child's trust and ability to trust and be connected. Familiarity feels friendly.

❖❖❖❖❖
Clever

Think before acting and after thinking the acting may not be necessary. Frequently we're reactive. We miss the clever possibilities that make our job easier and everybody's life more enjoyable. Helping children frame work, responsibility, boundaries and honesty in a different light, can make a difference in how they respond to us and what we expect. Remember how Tom Sawyer got his friends to paint the fence. Reflecting the enjoyment of responsibilities is clever, a way to have them see the joy in work. Teaching responsibilities as a privilege earned rather than assigned engenders eagerness. A clever note or suggestion is so much more acceptable than an angry demand. Tell clever stories. Kids love them. Especially stories about clever kids or clever things you did as a kid. The best stories though, are the ones telling of clever things they did when younger. Affirm their cleverness when they show it. Even the word "clever" is sort of funny and kind of clever.

❖❖❖❖❖
Creative

Create opportunities for pleasure, noticing, artistic expression, physical exertion, social opportunities, learning and travel. Nurture our own creative juices to model creativity. Be creative in our child care approach with joint decisions, switching places, jobs, role playing scenes, gentle mimicry. Value creativity and imagination. What can you do with a box, a newspaper, duct tape? Build a city or repair a train - straws, mud, leaves, clothes, all can stimulate creativity and build on the most precious human gift of all, imagination. Playing dress-up, drawing together, even 'Pictionary', write stories and jokes and share them. Remember our children will often become what we imagine them to be, they will always become what they imagine themselves to be. We are all ongoing products of our self creativity. Creativity and imagining come naturally to children, invite our children to teach us. Let the student be the teacher so we can discover our own childness.

❖❖❖❖❖
Consequential

Punishment and discipline seldom have a positive impact. Our children are not here to be controlled and molded. Notice, allow, and occasionally set up consequences. Most behaviors have consequences built into the behavior. It might be a feeling of shame, or getting in trouble with someone else, losing or breaking something, poor grades, loss of privileges in settings other than home. As a parent, teacher or care giver it's more important to notice the consequences than remove them. Removing them can be enabling and disrespectful. Our job is to notice the consequence and connect it to the behavior. This is how we learn. Almost every action has built in consequences. If there doesn't seem to be one, we may have to provide it. Losing a driving privilege for driving recklessly, losing kitchen privileges for not participating in food preparation or clean up. Enforcement of consequences can be time consuming so be careful of consequences you will not or cannot enforce or follow up on. Children can have a savings account and earn money and this money can be used to pay for treats as well as damages. Being removed from a setting is a possible consequence of anti-social behavior, or the withholding of noticing and affection for a temporary period. Use these sparingly for they engender shame. Approach the child with an intent to learn, not to punish or isolate. Children are not different than adults, just less experienced. As adults, we have consequences to our failures or poor behaviors, children need essentially the same. Abuse equipment and lose its use or do extra maintenance on it. Do some bartering, 30 days or 30 dollars, do the time or pay the fine. Allowing choices of consequences can be useful in allowing children to feel they have an impact on their lives and still have freedom.

Calm

S tay calm, except when it's incongruent to stay calm. Remember real crises are rare. When the setting and our feelings suggest excitement, show it. When our excitability or panic will frighten children even more in a situation, show calm. If they break something, if they hurt themselves, the car breaks down on the freeway, we get a speeding ticket or lose something, the calmer we are, the less anxious, frightened, or angry those around us will be. Soothing, calm words in a touchy setting can help children get through the setting. To be calm is not to be passive. Our calming is a salve for the anxiety and hurts of our children. When nothing else seems to be working, and all else fails, breathe. Calming others can be a way of calming ourselves. Calm yourself and find support. Calm does not mean never showing feelings. Our fear, anger and sadness are as important to model as joy and serenity. Calm is removing the panic or rage from an emotionally laden process.

❖❖❖❖❖
Capable

We demonstrate how we are capable by how we handle situations, help with directions and find information. Having information is much less important than knowing how to find it. When we see our children as capable, and provide opportunities for them to show their 'stuff', they become more sure of themselves. Children will do it when they are ready, not necessarily when they are capable of it. The more we push, the greater the likelihood of them not being ready. The roller coaster looks pretty scary to a child. It may be safe and we know it's safe, but it's important to give them the space to accept the risk involved in getting on it. Given space and opportunity our children will discover what they can do. Our children are capable of some things we can't do and never could do, but our children are not capable or ready for all the things we could do as children or as adults. Each persons capabilities and timing are part of their uniqueness.

We all have gifts. When we see other people sharing and speaking of their gifts, without bragging, without exaggeration, just reflecting the gift is there, it's easier to pull our gifts out to enjoy and share. We need to provide opportunities for our children to show what they are capable of doing as well as model our strengths and share our talents. Do not over- pressure them, or expose them to the evaluation, ridicule or approval of a lot of other people unless they decide they are ready.

❖❖❖❖❖
Connected

K eep the connection with spouse or primary relationship and other adult relationships as well as with children. Connecting with one should not mean disconnecting from others. We stay connected by being available wherever we are or whatever we are doing. Our availability is as important as our presence.

Connecting is done with notes and letters and calls - through hope, puppy wrestling, a wink, a hand on the shoulder. Connection is the antidote for shame. We can connect through shared entertainment, meals, games, discussions and in silence. Some of the most powerful connecting is done in silence.

Much of parenting is a process of making connections - or linking. We link the consequences of behavior to the behavior, we link the behavior to the feelings engendering the behavior, we link the feelings to what the feelings are a reaction to. This connecting helps children feel connected rather than disconnected. It enables the awareness of the chain of actions, feelings, behaviors and consequences.

Rather than telling or expecting a child to do something, keep the connection by doing it with them. This makes the experience more meaningful and joyful. Connect with other parents and share horrors, stories and joys. Connect to self and notice our feelings and actions as guides, connect to belief and spiritual values and reflect the connections in how we live.

❖❖❖❖❖
Competent

To show children the areas of life we are competent in, our work, building, talking, selling, teaching, we need to include them in the parts of our life where we show or do hobbies, sports, work or whatever. Children seldom see adults in the places where they are the most competent and have a difficult time respecting them because of it.

We must treat children as competent. Give them affirmation, and opportunities for success so they can discover and enjoy their competencies. If athletics is their bag, give them slack in other areas. Don't push too much for grades. One child may have poise, another perception, another persuasion. And they'll develop these in different areas. We can help provide the arena but we can't always provide the competence since it commonly comes from within. We can model competencies, expose children to the competencies of others and give them an opportunity to reach towards it, teaching them most competency is based on practice, work, and a sense of joy in the experience. Competency mostly is a product of the energy expended in developing it.

If we reflect our competency as care givers, we don't have to be defensive or arrogant, our children will reflect our competence in their relationship with themselves and their children. Included in competence is the ability to make mistakes and ask questions. With children, provide and utilize training, practice and learning opportunities, but not as a substitute for the free time where they can discover themselves and their areas of interest.

❖❖❖❖❖
Confidence

Be self assured, without a narcissistic ego. Our self confidence enables us to take risks, be ridiculous, sublime, poetic, or to sing, dance, play, giggle and take on projects. We teach children to have confidence, first by modeling it and then by having confidence in them. When they hesitate to try something, affirm we believe they would do fine and enjoy it and they may decide to wait for another time when they will do fine and enjoy it. When they are in a slump, don't minimize the slump, but tell stories of our great slumps, or zero for thirty, or the slumps of great people and how they dealt with it. Babe Ruth hit more home runs *and* struck out more often than anybody. Show confidence by keeping them in the line up, helping them practice, get tutoring and coaching, or even allowing them to take time out, or switch endeavors with the possibility of coming back to this one. Treat them the way you would like to be treated, now and as a child. Don't over rate confidence. Having confidence in oneself is sometimes less important than the willingness to take risks and risk failure.

Keep confidences, not secrets. Don't humiliate or shame, by telling on them, especially in front of their friends, your friends or other family members, strangers or acquaintances. Respect them and their feelings. Their confidence in us is a reflection of ours in them, ours in ourselves and our ability to keep their confidence. Reflect not on their failures, but on their effort and willingness to risk.

Credible

Keep your believability. Don't make rash promises, commitments or threats you can't or don't want to keep. Be true to your word, and when you must change your mind, break a promise or commitment, apologize and make amends. Sometimes we can offer a substitute or replacement, other times we can only give an explanation or an apology. Remember an amend is not about words, it's about change. Don't try to remove the feeling responses to a broken promise. Notice the feeling and explain your position. Do restitution where needed. Don't allow yourself to be perpetually punished or emotionally battered. To maintain credibility, you may need to take time outs before deciding something or before reacting to something. It's OK to move on to something else, or be willing to stay and hear it out. Be willing to fight about an issue, but listen to both sides rather than always falling on one side or the other.

Sometimes credibility is achieved by being incredible - even ridiculous.   Kids love to hear exaggerated stories, unbelievable stories, incredible experiences. It's important not to try to make the incredible, credible. Fantasy fuels imagination and creates a wonder of possibilities, but fantasy must be presented as fantasy. We can present fantasy as symbol and confirm children's fantasies while allowing them time to decide whether it's fantasy or reality.

❖❖❖❖❖

Coherence and Clarify

Sometimes when we're upset or overwhelmed, we speak to our children in gibberish or partial thoughts and sentences. When we're focused on other things we may do the same. We may be able to babble with friends, but child raising needs to be done with coherent words, phrases, and directions. Treat their excitable moments and incoherence with patience and gentle questioning.   Children often speak in parallels and parables. Look beyond the words and description for the real issues.

Our words and our lives may reflect incoherence. When we bounce from one thing to another, we seem to value something at one time and not at another. This lack of continuity, coherence and cohesion in our own lives might become acted out by our children. When we reflect a coherence of our values and beliefs, as well as words, our children's lives will also reflect coherence.

To be clear and to make things clear can prevent crisis and power struggles. Give clear directions on what we want done, and clear messages of what we expect. We may negotiate, compromise and change, and still remain clear with the process of our evolving decisions. To provide clarity for their binds, dilemmas and struggles is an essential of healthy parenting. Reflecting back with clear pictures or descriptions, what you see in them, their conflicts, and situations is more powerful than finding an answer or direction for them to take. Clarify by noticing what they feel, what you remember, heard or know, what they're saying, or what you can tell of them. In exposing their binds or dilemmas, you might say, "So if you go on the trip with Tom, Joe will be mad, and if you don't Tom will be upset. Seems as though you're in a tough spot." You might then ask, "what could you do that would make you feel the best about you?" The clarity may expose the real feeling underneath all the dilemmas. The clarity might expose the child's anger at being put in the bind. Clarity is the access to insight giving us the opportunity to make decisions and understand motivations.

❖❖❖❖❖

Concise

Keep it simple and specific. Rather than a big harangue, about the towels on the bathroom floor, just say "the towels." It's less shaming and easier to respond to. We don't get paid overtime for long lectures, so why bother? Brevity is an adult's salvation and helps prevent children from becoming defensive. Moving back to clever, a little note pinned to the towel, "hang me up so I can dry up" is another possibility.

Non-specific and over long directions are impossible to follow. They create anxiety and insecurity and move children towards apathy and hostility. Short notes get read, brief messages heard. We'll keep this one short and concise!

❖❖❖❖❖
Cooperation

Rather than telling them to do it, or doing it for them, do it with them sometimes. Some things seem overwhelming to children. The lawn, their room, the dishes, homework, learning a skill, drawing a map, traveling across town. Whenever possible, our willingness and availability to do it with them, lets them know they can depend on us, reduces the overwhelm, and gets it done. Usually at some point, they will let us know they want to do it themselves, or finish it themselves. We then can move on to our own projects, but let them know we're available if they need help, or if they'd like us to check with them later.

Adults teach cooperation by modeling it in adult relationships more than with children. Cooperative ownership of certain things should be balanced with individual rights and ownership. When both exist, children learn boundaries and sharing. Respect children's wishes not to share some toys. Have some toys specifically for sharing. Parents also need to model a cooperation involving relationships with school and community as well as extended family. Some family decisions can be cooperative around purchases, vacations, home improvements and the family rules. Parents model cooperation in their relationship with each other - single, married, separated or divorced.

❖❖❖❖❖
Co-parenting

The sooner our children are involved in their parenting, the better able they'll be to take care of themselves and care for others. Co-parenting doesn't mean they parent siblings, although their voluntary help with siblings is a privilege of responsibility and a co-parenting role. Co-parenting is their involvement in the decisions and process of their own parenting needs - their help in selection of consequences, priorities, religious practice, how they keep their room, curfews and so on. Co-parenting is essential for adolescence. We must involve them in the parenting process. This is not abrogating parental responsibility, it's enjoying the fruits of healthy parenting and avoiding power struggles. *Adolescents fire parents who don't retire.* To stay in control of a child until they're ready to leave home, then opening the door and saying "you're on your own, make your own decisions" is like keeping someone in a prison all their life, then opening the prison door and saying good-bye, and watching the person get run over by a truck because they don't know how to cross the street safely. Integrated into the process of growing up children need life skills and preparation for making their own decisions.

Choices

Alternatives. Freedom is the ability to choose, to make choices. To do this we need information and support. Children often hear no or yes, but seldom get to decide. So much of adulthood is looking at and choosing between several alternatives, constantly making choices. Many of us are unprepared for adulthood because of parents who didn't allow choice or provide alternatives. Positive binds provide a choice for either decision to come out positively. "Would you like to put your crayons away now or after your snack?" Offering alternatives about jobs, consequences, treats and travel, helps children feel affirmed and important, and teaches them responsibility. It's important not to overwhelm with excess combinations, choices and alternatives, but provide real choice according to developmental and chronological age. Clothes, hair, their room, privacy, grades, sports, play, friends are all important choices children make. Don't try to control what you can't control.

Provide an environment for choosing. When we pressure children into something or out of something, they're more likely to react with the opposite. If we believe music is important, and we decided that our children will learn to play an instrument, it's important to at least allow them to decide which musical instrument they would like to study, and maybe even how many times a month or week they would like to take lessons. What sort or practice schedule would they like to set up? Evenings, or afternoons or week ends, etc.? Once they have made the choice, the responsibility for follow-up becomes much easier, it's internal, it's built into the decision and their choice. If we provide parental pressure the pressure is for following up on choices they've made, not the choices we made. *Guiding is not pressuring.*

❖❖❖❖❖
Competitive Spirit

Teaching competition can be touchy; some of us are much better at it than others. (Just kidding!) Seriously, teaching children to compete, to be able to make the choice of doing the best they can is wonderful. Teaching them to be competitive to win or feel good about themselves at the expense of others is destructive. To be able to compete without being competitive is the goal and is taught by how we compete and by feeling good about ourselves in what we do. Competing is being able to select the areas we will work at excelling and doing our best. Vote no on the phrase "whatever you do is OK, honey, as long as you always do your best." Or "anything worth doing is worth doing well." We all need to select when to do our best. And we need to do some things for the sheer pleasure of it, or simply to participate, whether we do it well or poorly. A competitive spirit will be reflected in enjoying the game, not the outcome. It'll show up in areas of our life we decide to invest our time and energy while moving towards excellence.

❖❖❖❖❖
Cherishing

Always be mindful of how precious both children and childness is. Cherish the moments, the movements, the needs, the problems, the growing, the cuteness, the bratiness. Cherish the sacred calling we have as guardians of the most precious of all creatures we will encounter, a young human life. We can cherish our children more easily when we embrace and cherish our own childness. It helps to keep a perspective knowing some of the most precious moments we'll look back on will be everyday things, some of the hard things, it might even be a fight over a silly little thing. It may be a time when things seemed hopeless, or an evening when we held our child's hand when they had a fever. It may be the joy of watching them compete in an area of their choice. Cherishing is holding value. If we value and cherish our children, they'll be a priority and we'll be involved. Many of us need reminders of cherishing as we go about our busy schedules.

❖❖❖❖❖
Childlike

In parenting, we must be childlike, not childish. In becoming childlike we notice with awe the lives we protect, we maintain the wonder, curiosity, noticing and creativity towards the world and others. Through this we can give our child permission to grow in their childness and bring it intact into their adulthood and future families. Touching our childlike needs, finding our support, affirming our vulnerability as well as the needs of our children teaches them how to reach out. Embracing our interdependency enables our children to discover interdependence with others and the world. Interdependence is our ability to depend on others and allow others to depend on us without us losing our sense of self. It also fuels us for the meeting of their dependency needs. Not by over focusing on them but with a benign availability. Care givers need to be on call. Children will teach us to move back to the noticing and wonder of childness. They can teach us to be feeling, to trust, question and be playful. Play is the work of children. We are all children. Again, growing up is childness entering adulthood where we don't lose childness, but gain adulthood.

Character

We would rather be characters than build character! Much damage is done in the name of character building. Abuse such as hitting, yelling or excess pressure doesn't build character, it destroys it. Children will have deep character when they see us model values, having shared goals, and living a life with priorities. Integrity is taught as boundaries and honesty are taught. When we have integrity, our children choose it for themselves.

Character is a part of personality development. Each child has characteristics that when affirmed and channeled become strengths, and when not, may become destructive. Through these characteristics, we can enjoy the uniqueness of our children, while remembering childhood is change. Do not script children according to the specific characteristics we see in a particular developmental stage. Be a character, reflect your character, know and enjoy your unique characteristics and your children will follow, or not, depending on their character. It's also enjoyable if we have interesting characters in our life who children can learn from, to discover the differences in the world and its people.

❖❖❖❖❖
Chronicle

We are the historians and chroniclers of our children's childhood. This childhood is entrusted to us to be delivered back to them in the form of stories, photos, memorabilia. We can't save everything or remember all but we can save landmark moments and examples of work and play from each childhood period. Recording through films - video or photos, provides an incredible replay but the stories and words are equally, if not more, important. Journaling, telling the stories in writing is a record for the re-telling, a treasure chest of the past. Remembering pets, friends, foods, favorite songs, special times, special gifts given and received, adventures and misadventures, holidays, tricks, favorite games, sports and the incredible imaginary creations of childhood mean childhood will never be lost for us or our children.

When traveling, keep a trip log. Travel can be high adventure for children with new sights, smells, people and play. Chronicle the relationships and adventures of adults as well. Our journey is a story, the sense of our history to build identity and maintains integrity.

❖❖❖❖❖
Cooking

Cook up some excitement. Cook together and make it a family affair. Offer recipes for various eyes - meals done cooperatively and play cooking too. Allowing children to participate as they show interest invites them to belong in the family food process. It will usually be messier and take longer and there'll be times it won't work out but it could offer lots of fun and learning.

Cooking can teach nutrition, the need for food cleanliness, how to tidy up as well as be a creative bonding time. We can model a healthy relationship with food - enjoying it without the fear of gaining weight or being over rigid about what to eat or not to eat. When children first want to join in they're usually satisfied with simply stirring and licking the bowl! It's often easier to invite them along than saying no and keeping them at bay. Being able to cook gives children a sense of independence, confidence and responsibility. It's an outlet for creative expression and challenge. Cooking can be about treats, kooky cooking, designing cooking or just cooking up some jokes!

❖❖❖❖❖
Coordinate

P rioritize, keep the flow. Parenting is like running a business. Coordinate meals, work schedules, vacations, parental availability, time spent along with individual members and as a family. Coordinate parenting jobs according to time, talents, experiences and even some according to whose children are whose. Parents need not always coordinate a united front. It really isn't helpful if they do. Their disagreement and how these are dealt with include some of the most important aspects of learning about fighting. (See the 36 guidelines for conflict resolution in this series.) Meals can be coordinated to share and everyone invited without rigidity. Being late consistently is generally passive-aggressive. This passive anger may come from over structuring, over scheduling or over coordinating. Free time is a time for growing.

Coordinate physically by offering physical challenges, playing physically with children, modeling and coordinating physical activities, noticing the grace or fluidity of the child, not the mistakes, offering space and applauding for physical energy and effort. Offer lessons in skill building and prioritize with the child. Be involved, but not overly so. Balance is the key.

❖❖❖❖❖
Conserving

Conserve traditions, history, rituals and values. Values are conserved by modeling what we value not enforcing what we think should be valued. Affirming when we see other family members reflecting a value, noticing and giving the value a name is a true conservation of spirituality. Conserve energy. Yours and the power companies! Conserve resources. Model a low consumptive approach to life. Packaging waste, recycling, appreciating the wilderness and working to conserve it.

Rituals are an important part of conserving. Some of the things children complain loudest about today become the things they cherish the most later. "What, it's the third week of August, of course we're going on vacation, what a drag! Always up to the lake, always to the cabin." But later on, they talk with fondness about how the third week of August we always spent a family week at the cabin. The popcorn and movie on Friday nights, the 20 minutes before dinner playing outside, Saturday drives, Sunday church and breakfast, seasonal sports, holiday traditions. All these repetitive family activities may draw these complaints but can be cherished memories we look back to. Rituals should be available, not rigid. Not so everyone must participate in the same way each time. Stories about parents, grandparents, other relatives and friends are also ways of conserving richness of family. Our history is held in slide carousels, boxes of photos, journals, diaries, memorabilia, but mostly in the minds and hearts of family members.

Change

B eing flexible will keep us from getting bent out of shape. The one constant in life is change. Children change faster than seasons. Enjoy and savor each stage and be ready with open arms, minds, and hearts for the next. Many of us are afraid of the changes we see. Especially adolescence! We can show concern in a mild caring way, but trying to stop or control change is like harnessing a tornado. The best we can do, sometimes, is head for shelter. Their values are intact if they have them. We can't protect them from every one of life's possibilities, but we can see when the change is a danger sign.

When too many changes come too fast, children may go on overload, become depressed, possibly suicidal, develop stress disorders, and illness or become chemically dependent just as adults do. We can't always know if they are running into bullies in school, (teachers or students) or elsewhere. We can't always see when the pressure is too great, forces too many, but we can notice and monitor and record their changes. Change is a normal reflection of childhood, but change for the worse can be a sign of trouble. Look for changes in grades, friends, affect, sleep, sibling relationships, exploration, privacy, agitation, interests, pets. If there are changes in all of the above, it's probably puberty. Other things to look for: drugs, sexual fears, bullying, abuse, a mistake or an accident coming back to haunt, depression, suicidal intention, statements about life not being worth living. If they've endured a catastrophe, a violent act, a trauma, loss or accident of any type, it's important to notice change and to relate the change back to the event they've endured and give them a chance to do more debriefing of the event. Look not only at the child, but at the family, the marriage, our lives. Children often reflect our changes, especially the covert ones we are not dealing with so well.

❖❖❖❖❖

Confidants

Children need confidants. Children may confide in us as parents, but our relationship with them has limitations, and we need to accept there'll be hills and valleys. They won't always want to approach us and won't always be able to. Our ability and willingness to help find and notice the possibilities of an outside confidant is healthy parenting. An aunt, an uncle who can relate, a grandparent, family friend, neighbor, teacher, coach, therapist, pastor, rabbi, youth minister, can all serve as a confidant.

When children are being threatened or hurt, the need to talk to someone about what's going on and their feelings may be more important than changing the threat or hurt. The ability to debrief the incident and feeling is a primary factor in how the abuse or incident may impact their present or future lives. The closer to the time of the incident they're able to share with someone, generally the less impact the incident will have on their lives.

Confidants are also helpful for getting advise and support on puberty, sexual changes, physical concerns, relationship issues, and just growing up. For children, especially in early adolescence, to be able to share with confidants, other children or adults, things they can not comfortably talk to parents about is normal. Parents who get into tell me all, seldom allow for privacy and the natural process of separation from parents and entry into the world.

Celebrate

The posture of celebrating life is challenging to maintain. We do our daily grinds, traffic, bills, calls returned, time demands. If we take a little time to move into a mode of seeing through the eyes of childness, the splendor of the gift of life and of the planet, it can renew us for the next onslaught of demands and stresses. To watch parents celebrate life can have more impact on children than a trip to Disney World. Not that parents can't celebrate life at Disney World. Childhood is marked by celebrations, birthdays, holidays, commencements, anniversaries, weddings, family gatherings. Include children in the planning, give them space and a part in the celebration, without being the complete focus, unless it's their occasion.

Children learn from adult play and celebrations. It's important to model celebrating and play without drug use. Non-alcoholic parties are difficult for many parents, but if we really expect our children to not use drugs, we must model the abstinence we want them to have. Nicotine and alcohol are both addictive and terminal drugs causing chemical dependency. Dancing, special treats, special friends, music, gifts, games, movement, fireworks, surprises, rides, clowns, magicians, singing, picnics, sports and chatting are the stuff of celebrations. Renting a cotton candy machine, making ice cream, regular or balloon volley ball, a sprinkler, a kiddy pool full of water (not beer), water balloons and blowing bubbles, endless possibilities of safe fun are available for celebrations.

Creating the celebration is part of the celebration. Birthdays are important. They don't need to be over done, but noticing and attention on a birthday, our unique celebration day, gives us the reality of being noticed and cared about. We like celebrating solstices, applauding sunsets. We always plan on celebrating the completion of a book. But it seems books are never quite completed. Maybe we'll celebrate when we hit the "Times" best seller list. Tell your friends to buy this book so we can celebrate!

❖❖❖❖❖
Compromise

If we bend, we don't break. Flexibility, a mark of a healthy person, requires compromise. Our fears can set us up to be brittle and rigid. We have ideas of how things ought to be, often based on how they were in our childhood. We may enforce these, not recognizing children are different, times are different, and our childhood might not have been so hot anyway.

When we compromise, we don't compromise ourselves or our values, we enforce the value of cherishing change and embracing the uniqueness of the people, time and situation we are in. Don't compromise on health and safety. Most of the rest is negotiable. We're not recommending being a patsy, always giving up or giving in, we do recommend listening to reason and reasons and giving alternatives a hearing while using judicious evaluation. Because I told you so is a parent cop out. Listening ad infinitum to declarations of unfairness and children's complaints is a parent burn-out. In between is setting a time allowance for discussion, giving a decision time to think over and affirming the child's position through the process. Even a statement of "I wish I could do it the way you would like me to" can be helpful, or "you deserve what you're asking for, I just can't provide it now." It's as important children learn delayed gratification as it is for them to know their wishes and wants are heard and respected.

❖❖❖❖❖
Chat and Communicate

Talking is only one aspect of family communication. Certainly talking over decisions, the future, the past, directions, problems, addictions, illness and relationship issues are important. Denial and not talking about problems causes lower functioning families. Problems don't make a low functioning family, the inability to acknowledge, discuss the problem or the feelings about the problem or responses to the problem does. We need to communicate what's going on in a way children can understand and hear without being overly frightened, overwhelmed or feeling responsible. Communicate in a style and with quality information appropriate for the child's age and development. (see Pathways To Intimacy with 36 Guidelines for Communicating.)

Chatting, the ability to socialize, breeds self esteem. Small talk is a prerequisite to friendship and intimacy. To be able to chat about sports, current events, the weather, politics, business, even media and entertainment enables us to socialize with enough people to select those we want to deepen our communication and experience with. Social chatting skills enable us to find a group, a culture, friends without having to act out, use drugs or find a cult to feel belonging. Small talk is often put down but is a way of bridging and helps social discussion become a safe process. Gradually moving from chatting to deeper self disclosure, marked with building trust is a way of maintaining boundaries and choices.

❖❖❖❖❖

Community

To model community and sharing, a sense of the oneness we have with other people, with life, with our planet is the highest and most sacred function of parenting. We do this by showing and speaking of our respect for life and the environment, doing works of service, and giving. Sometimes involve children or at least invite them along without forcing and affirm their sharing and giving.

Participating in sacrifice and sharing, the feeling coming from sacrifice, will spark a caring sense of community. We also need to teach limits on sacrifice. To model giving from what we have, not out of our emptiness. We need to teach the dignity in accepting help from others when we have needs as well as humility in helping others when they have needs. By how we view and take care of our family, our communities, our schools and countries, we can break down the parochialism and prejudices our children will encounter causing and coming out of fear and insecurity.

Respect for the earth is taught by respect for property and not over owning or over consuming. Teaching what we have comes from the earth at a price, and we must pay the price and give back to the earth. To teach and notice consequences is the prime element in teaching earth stewardship. Do family recycling, not as a nuisance or requirement but as a joyful activity. Using parks, providing wilderness experiences, joining community celebrations and attending school and community events help children respect the sense of community, the communal aspects of their living, of their life.

Allowing a balance between ownership and sharing of personal and family resources models community responsibility as well. Teaching loanership over ownership, what we have and our involvement with people is not a permanent fixture. We don't own people, relationships, community, the earth. It's all on loan for our protecting and enjoying.

❖❖❖❖❖

Kindness

OK it's not a C. We said be consistent, not predictable! It could have been a C word. Being kind, not wimpy or retiring, just kind. "When we are kind and real, our children will be kind and real." When we are kind and unrealistic, our children will rebel against kindness.

Kind isn't a denial of the meanness in people. It doesn't mean never getting angry, or saying or doing nasty things. It's re-membering what's important. It's making restitution and amends, being willing to change and realizing how precious and fragile are the lives entrusted to us. We can be mindful of the impact of our words, looks and behaviors on those around us. Adults often minimize the impact of anger or violence on children. Kind doesn't conquer or cure. It helps our children feel safe and respected.

Being kind to ourselves and other adults, especially if we're in a marriage or significant relationship is as important to our chil-dren as being kind to our children. Kind is a part of kinder, the German word for children. It's a kindred spirit we share in childness with all persons. With kindness we kindle the warmth of friendship on our orbiting, kinder-garden, earth.

For anyone who wants a 36th "C" we offer Candid. We have tried to be candid about parenting and care giving. It can be one of the most joyful of all journeys and wrought with pain and insecurity. Many of us have attempted to parent without having had parenting. Quite candidly, the most important step in being able to give it is to find it. If not from parents, then from people around us. We cannot write checks out of an empty account. Find people who will notice, who will be there to support us, who cherish us on our journey.

The Sacred Trust

❖ ❖ ❖

PART TWO

❖ ❖ ❖

THE GRACE OF BELONGING
Creating Families of Wellness and Joy

The Grace of Belonging
Creating Families of Wellness and Joy

Introduction

"A high functioning family is found by learning and working in a community of friendship. We are grown in family of origin, we continue growing in family of creation."

An African proverb says that it takes an entire village to raise a child. A family may be the foundation for individual development but community is the basis for family development. Family values are not a substitute for a fractured society and a lost sense of community. Community support and awareness of individual needs is as important to children as are nurturing parents. We are all responsible for all children.

Families have been under much pressure. For many years people have focused on dysfunctional families, claiming that all families are dysfunctional and if we don't recognize the dysfunction we are in denial. All families function. Some families are higher functioning, some are lower functioning and most are a blend of functioning levels. Maybe it is better understood that all families have problems. How we handle a problem is a reflection of how functioning we are at a particular time.

Whether we were hurt in our families or not - it is in our families of origin we learn how to cope with being hurt. Our ability to move through the grieving process, protect ourselves, assert needs and sustain intimacy is primarily a product of family influence.

Family experience is probably the most important process in our life. In the context of our family we move through developmental stages, building on the strengths of one attribute and gaining another. One of the better known theories of developmental stages was presented by Erik Erikson. He believed the progression began in babyhood with developing *trust* and then *autonomy*; in childhood gaining initiative and next industry; during adolesence developing *identity*, and then *intimacy*; in adulthood the stages being *generativity* and finally *integrity*. Having an environment of safety, trust, and nurturing complimented with challenges and being affirmed give us the spring board to travel through our developmental stages. When these attributes are learned in family, we can carry them into all relationships and other systems we find ourselves in as adults.

In family we can learn to work with others while maintaining our uniqueness. This balance of expressing one's self and compromising within a system to maintain healthy connection and functioning is finding self esteem while valuing others and their needs.

Families offer a place to learn about communication, move through difficult times, resolve conflict and hopefully energize our discovery of intimacy. An important relationship in family - the foundation - is the parents relationship. Watching our parent's model healthy intimacy in their adult relationships is how we learn intimacy - this is true whether our parents are married to each other or not. Parent's healthy adult intimacy is more important than parents being intimate with children. When parent's relationship breaks down, the parents often reach to children for affectional and support needs. Children are not there to meet the needs of parents but parents need to be there to meet the needs of children and allowing them a process of discovery of self sufficiency.

Sometimes when parents were neglected in their families, they over focus on kids and cowntinue self and relationship neglect causing inadequate modeling for children to learn about intimacy and self care. All too often parents *use* children as objects of rage, frustration and for affectional needs or to be or do the things that they couldn't be, to give their lives meaning.

Our children are not *of us*, *for us*, or *about us*. We don't own our children, they are the miracle of the gift of life itself. We cannot appreciate the miracle of our children until we can embrace the miracle of our childness.

Have you ever found people with whom you felt safe enough to be yourself? People who accepted you for who you are, believed in you while nurturing your journey? A family brought us to life, a family brings us to life. In family we learn to live and play, love and pray. Family are the people we can always come home to.

Our roots are planted in family - of *origin* or *creation*. When we are firmly grounded we can spread our wings and soar. The following suggestions for healthy family life are taken from the illustrated gift book <u>*Roots and Wings*</u>. Each suggestion has been expanded and will hopefully provide insight and guidance for the journey of family. Following are ideas for creating a family of awareness and care with elements on living, loving, and exploring with others!

Suggestions for Creating Families of Wellness and Joy

❖❖❖❖❖❖
Listen with your eyes

Eye contact is the connecting point of communication. How often have loved ones shared with us while we continued to watch TV or read the newspaper. Glancing away is a sign of shutting down. The one sharing with us may become more demanding and frantic in response to our disconnecting. In our eyes we can reflect the care and acceptance that allows a sense of completion for the sharing. Our eyes can speak our response of love and attentiveness, an affirmation more than words.

❖❖❖❖❖❖
Listen to their eyes

In the eyes of those around us is the truth of their needs, the honesty of their noticing. The eyes are the windows to the soul and in looking at the eyes, we can notice the soul, whether it is safe or tormented, joyous or hurtful. The eyes tell of shame and dishonesty as well as truth and love. Responding to the eyes is deeper than responding to words and actions. The sparkle and mischievousness of their eyes can spark the magic in our lives.

Laugh at the sound of laughter

Laughter and glee tend to surround children in safe settings as well as adults with certain friends and times. When we hear laughter, rather than allow it to irritate and grate on our present mood, how much easier to enter its envelope and deliver us into the glee of its source. If we are open to the possiblity hearing the laughter itself is usually humorous enough to set our own chuckles in motion.

Embrace differences

Each person has their own path. Sometimes the path may parallel our expectations and overlap our own but it is still their path with different forks, branches, dips and directions. Sameness is not a virtue. The noticing, affirming and allowing differences to grow creates the strength and true wealth of a family. Different beliefs are difficult to accept but often the difference is a step toward something greater or an integration of beliefs producing deeper integrity. Different dreams, language, lifestyle, friends and pleasures can be embraced and learned from when they are not destructive. Resolving differences is the predecessor to cherishing and embracing them.

❖❖❖❖❖
Acknowledge strengths

People grow best when their strengths are noticed rather than their flat spots. Improvements come easily when our values and goals are supported even though they may seem remote at the time. Change comes more easily when we are affirmed for what we are and why we are there, when the strength of the present posture is noticed and valued. Each one of us has our own area of genius and creativity that when acknowledged makes even the hard parts easier. Helping family members find their successes is the job of the entire family.

❖❖❖❖❖
Affirm uniqueness

The affirming of uniqueness is best when directed toward internals rather than externals. Clothes, style and accomplishment can be noticed but a person is deeper. *Affirm what you can't photograph* - the sparkle in one's eye, a sense of humor and laughter, a spirit and guardianship, imagination and creativity, the bounce in one's step, the grace of action all belong uniquely to the individual. To notice is the connection to the person, not what they do or wear.

❖❖❖❖❖❖
Read aloud, read alone

Being read to provides a sense of warmth and care. The attention is given to us but isn't on us. The context of the reading enriches and stimulates imagination, creates a craving and curiosity for more. It teaches communication and verbal skills and best of all feels cozy. The world is introduced into the fertility of imagination in the reading so much more so than the electronic baby sitter of TV. Reading on our own gives us a refueling and provides a modeling. It is a personal activity done without breaking off community. It can be restful, stimulating and growthful all at once. Reading provides exercise, adventure and risk taking for the mind and soul.

❖❖❖❖❖❖
Breed music

Music is the movement of the human spirit. To be introduced to music at an early age deepens and strengthens the spirit. Provide variety and opportunity to play, sing and listen. We are all musicians and singing is to speaking as inhaling a fragrance is to breathing. Don't fight family choices on music or musical instruments. Introduce your own and blend. Music is an expression of culture, love, rebellion, pain and joy, plus many others. The highest moments of humanity are shown in the music that comes from the universal harmony of spirit. Model music to teach music.

❖❖❖❖❖❖
Give time, take time

Time is a valuable and often scarce commodity in family. Children need our availability, not just in quality but at certain stages and times, quantity as well. Couples need time to maintain and build intimacy as well as resolve differences. With all the time demands and multiple needs it is easy to miss taking the time we need for refueling, rest, recreation. The modeling of self care is still the most important gift we can give others. It teaches and offers permission for each family to do the same.

❖❖❖❖❖❖
Balance attention

Our attention, like time, also has limitations. At times different family members will need more attention than others. Some members may require more attention always. Certain members are easier to pay attention to and some create crises to find attention. Balance attention does not mean equal, but given the unique needs of each person we may plan and focus for a period on the person who may be less demanding, neglected, or harder to give to. Remember, balance means paying attention to us as well.

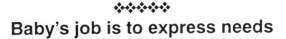

Baby's job is to express needs

Infants enter the world totally dependent but not uncommunicative. They generally do a good job of expressing what they need at any time, day or night, often in less than a pleasant matter - this is their job. The primary function is to let everyone and anyone know that a want or need exists at any given time. Children continue to express needs as they grow older, but often not so directly. Acting out, withdrawal, aggression and obnoxious behaviors are all expressions of needs. Reading beyond the behavior and looking at the need is a parenting requirement. Children do not distinguish between wants and needs. That job is for parents. Needs must be met, wants may be evaluated, meeting some, delaying some and denying some.

❖❖❖❖❖❖

Parents job is to listen to babies

The crying of an infant or the wailing of a small child are certainly not difficult to hear, but listening goes beyond what we hear to interpret the need, the source of the problem. It is a good idea to check out our own needs and feelings since children will often reflect and act out our hidden issues. Their cry can be an echo of the hurt and anger within us or our relationships. All parents become angry at the cries, demands and needs of their children. To listen to and talk about our feelings is the best prevention for lashing out and hurting the child with that anger.

❖❖❖❖❖❖
Kids hear and respond even if we do not think so

Children often seem not to hear us and they may pretend not to respond. Children hear not only what we say but how we say it and whether or not we really mean it. They always respond but one of their jobs is to not let adults know they responded or heard. When parents make suggestions or notice something eventually the suggestion will usually show up or the noticing will have an impact. As adults we get used to expecting immediate response and action or at least acknowledgment within a short period of time. This is not necessarily the way children, especially adolescents respond.

❖❖❖❖❖❖
Make believe

Imagination is a blend of creativity, hope, play, and learning. Children thrive on fantasy, stories, invented scenes and dramas. Pretending to be royalty, French, nomads, explorers, ranchers, space adventurers or animals. Pretending to be loving and happy can make us loving and happy. It is called "act as if." Pretending gives us a chance to experience, act, dramatize and express what often remains hidden within. It allows risk and teaches risk taking. Make believe helps build courage, as well as social and entertainment skills.

❖❖❖❖❖
Play dress up

Children and adults can enjoy playing dress up. Collect costumes - old or interesting. Store items of clothing, a collection of crazy hats is a hit at parties and gatherings for all ages. Costume parties need not be restricted to Halloween. Wearing crazy outfits is an adjunct to pretending and teaches drama and playfulness. When adults dress up, a new personality is often seen or perhaps it is a repressed part of the real personality. Looking silly and acting weird, or looking weird and acting silly can enliven and enrich the family adventure.

❖❖❖❖❖
Do picnics and parades

Picnics can be adventurous and nutritious, elaborate or simple. A picnic is an attitude more than a type of meal. Picnics can be in the rain or sun, they can be done outside or in any room of the house, they can be a part of a sporting event or they can be the sporting event itself. Pot luck picnics, deli picnics, fast food picnics, gourmet picnics, tail gate, beach, hiking, TV bedroom picnics all make the meal a little more fun. Parades simply involve a few people and a theme. Carrying a few stuffed animals around the block on Easter can be the First Stuffed Animal Easter Parade. A little music can liven a parade up. Bicycle parades, lawn parades, stroller parades, boat parades, everybody loves a parade and no family should be without at least one.

❖❖❖❖❖
Puppy wrestle

Human contact is like a growth hormone, tender, cuddling, holding and touching is not enough. Playful touch, gentle rough house, mock wrestling can be just as important. Watch chimps, cubs, monkeys, puppies and kittens. Some of the most loving moments occur with puppy wrestling. But remember that "stop." "enough," or "no" means "stop," "enough," or "no". And not too rough. Children will do their own puppy wrestling and often enjoy it when adults roll into the pile. If a member gets hurt, teach nurturing and accept it as part of the process without minimizing it. Have and maintain a safe environment for rough housing with soft floor covering, little furniture and no sharp edges, at least in some part of the house.

❖❖❖❖❖
Be consistent not predictable

Children and adults need consistency in their lives. Patterns, rituals, rhythms allow us to find a pace and operate in security. When something happens, an accident, a hurt or loss it is important for adults to respond as best they can in a manner consistent with responses to similar events of the past. Inconsistency of parental reactions is considered a stress producing process for children. Be consistent with limits, expectations, care and safety. Consistency does not mean predictability. The same words, overused rituals and limit setting set up anger and boredom. Newness and occasional surprise keep it interesting and a lot more fun.

❖❖❖❖❖
Be active not reactive

Many of us live life as a reaction to the expectations of others and events outside our control. We become parents and continue to react or to overreact. In this reactiveness we may over focus and spectate, even becoming hyper vigilant, losing a sense of self empowerment and awareness. We can give those we react to, especially children, too much control over our own lives. In becoming proactive we can be more creative. Proactive is anticipating and preventing a crisis that can control our lives and staying in touch with our own needs and reality through modeling, healthy self care. In learning pro-activity we no longer set up our children to have crises and tantrums to elicit our reactions or test our reactiveness.

❖❖❖❖❖
Allow consequences

Behavior is meaningful and is based on feelings. Some behavior is destructive and creates harm. Many of us as care givers are busy undoing, cleaning up and preventing the harm done from the behaviors of others. This type of care giving may be enabling. When a person does not experience and learn from the consequences of the behavior, they are all too likely to continue or escalate the behavior. As parents we seldom need to give consequences for inappropriate behavior since most of such behavior has a built in consequence. A respectful and educational approach is to notice when the consequence is present and link it to the behavior. The person creating the consequence is then allowed to deal with it within their limitations and support. Most of us need help in linking our consequences to the behaviors.

❖❖❖❖❖

Affirm feelings when you cannot affirm the behavior

Since not all behavior is okay, not all behavior can be affirmed. Since behavior is based on feelings, the feelings can be affirmed and noticed giving a greater choice about dealing with the feelings rather than acting them out. Just as we link the consequence to the behavior, we can link the behavior to the feelings. Often the feeling is understandable when we view the context, understanding what the feeling is a reaction to or how can the feeling be expressed in a different way. Feelings are gifts and guides, when we have guidance, noticing and affirmation of the feeling.

❖❖❖❖❖
Don't be mean

As obvious as this may seem, frequently we treat those closest to us with injustice, grumpiness or isolation and detachment.   This meanness usually has little to do with those around us. Rather it is our projection of emotional issues that come from other parts of our lives. Our grumpiness does have an impact. Too often we minimize the effect of our moods, anger and interactions on the people around us. Family members tend to internalize the reactions and attitude towards them. The meanness becomes a feeling of broken-ness, a damaged sense of self, a meanness towards self. It creates shame that can damage identity. When we are grumpy or feeling nasty it is best to acknowledge it but not project it onto people we care about.

❖❖❖❖❖
Don't be obscene

Obscenity is common enough in our culture. Our families should be safe harbors sheltering us from much of the crass and obscene in life. Obscene gestures, language and behaviors are not funny, nor are they a neces-sary part of family life. Language can be rich, explicit and honest without obscenities. Behavior need not be prudish and stilted but within a natural flow we can still be polite. The issue of what is obscene may need review. What is seen as obscene varies with cultures, socio-economics, eth-nic background, geography and individuals. Some of our sensibilities may not make much sense given our present life styles and culture but it is important to not let standards go just because they do not seem to fit in with the norm. The norm is not always healthy. Evaluate and gather, then shed what is excess baggage.

❖❖❖❖❖

Don't lean

Pressure is not all bad, with no pressure of any type some of us would flounder. The floundering is not necessarily so bad, but each of us wants to know how to push toward our strengths and some of us need a gentle nudge. Too much pressure is like leaning. It adds weight and slows us down, sometimes creating defiance and a refusal to move or budge. We lean when we over investigate, over lecture, over expect. Affirming the positive and allowing family members their weak areas or flat spots builds self esteem much more than "you can do it all" and "excel everywhere" messages. Leaning on children tends to knock them down as does pushing, prodding and pulling.

❖❖❖❖❖

Don't litter

Litter is not our major ecological concern but it is the easiest one to address that can make an immediate difference and teach an approach to the world suggesting respect and conserving. The production of trash as a part of consumption is the key to litter. Consume less and we litter less. Modeling a life style of produceing less litter and the appropriate recycling or disposing of this trash teaches children a respect for the planet and a sure inroad into building self respect in the child. Candy wrappers, gum, beverage containers and so on all have their place and this is one area where we get to be *picky*.

❖❖❖❖❖
Self disclose

Our family interacts on the basis of each person's feelings, thoughts, communication and behavior. When members are aware of the goings on with each other, their reactions do not seem so crazy or incomprehensible. The more they know, the less chance they will have to act out or be controlled by the struggles. We are resilient given information, but close off information and we will crack. We generally know what is going in our feelings and inner sense and when it is open we can plan our response and make choices. Sharing our losses, hurts, feelings, activities, frustrations, dreams, disappointments and fears can be done without dumping or expecting others to fix these. We need to share at a level and in a manner that is appropriate for the person we share with.

Let your family know who you are

Often we fail to tell the story of us to our family members. The story of our back ground is a fascinating tale. It is also the story of the background of our children. Who we are is in large part where we have been, including the family history, both sides. Experiences of our youth, past events, celebrations, trials, failures, experiences and disappointments help others know who we are and gives a better picture of who they are. Sometimes one side of the family is better known than the other, possibly because of a low functioning system or a deep rift in the family. The telling may expose us to painful memories and present hurts which are part of the ongoing story of us.

❖❖❖❖❖❖

Let your family know where you are

Our on going presence is not as important as our on going availability. Even leaving for a short time to run errands can create anxiety for family members if they do not know. Leaving notes reduces stress and fear. It also eliminates the issue of "did I or did I not" mention it. The notes facilitate our being found for emergencies and crises. We all need privacy but the need to be accountable and accessible need not interfere with our personal meanderings and needs. Often in stress or when travel becomes common place it takes an extra effort to keep the family informed of our whereabouts. Short notes on post notes, phone calls, messages left on answering machines or an itinerary all can contribute to a greater sense of family and security.

❖❖❖❖❖
Model emotional fluency

To be congruent is more reassuring than being nice and covering our feelings of anger or pain. Emotional fluency involves the use of feeling terms and the appropriate expression and suppression of our feelings. The fluency is having our outside expression of words and body language match our internal experience of what we are feeling. Feelings can be shared and spoken of without huge explosions and cathartic release. When the emotional response or event warrants something big it can still be done in safe and healthy settings. Emotional fluency is reassurance to others that we are dealing with the feelings. We can also model a request for support remembering adults need support from other adults and children supporting the emotional needs of parents should be done on a very limited basis.

❖❖❖❖❖
Sprinkle hope

Hope is a life preserver we can grasp when it feels like we are sinking. Sometimes it feels as though all we have left is hope and it becomes enough. Never take away hope for it is hope that our dreams catapult from. We can offer words of hope and encouragement without being a compulsive cheer leader or giving rise to unrealistic expectations and false hopes. Hope must be allowed to seep into cracks in the darkness. It is a ray of spiritual light inspiring us to rise above depression and apathy. Hope is holding on to value and belief in a creation of love, a belief of betterment. Little sprinkles of hope eventually wash away the dust of despair.

❖❖❖❖❖❖
Sparkle courage

Courage is sparked by courage modeled. It takes courage to reach out, be vulnerable, ask or share what is going on. Fear is the threshold of courage, we notice and listen to the fear to find the courage. There is little real intimacy outside of risk. Risk can be life enhancing when it comes from wisdom and healthy modeling. The ability to put oneself out there in creativity, humor, guardianship, ideas, writings, song, work, all come from modeled courage and support of mentors, parents, role models. Inspiration is the healthiest of all discipline techniques.

❖❖❖❖❖❖
Spackle confidence

We all have cracks and fissures. No surface on earth is perfectly flat or unmarked. To focus on the blemishes and fissures creates gaping holes or cracks in our ability to function, to relate well. Encouragement and affirmation is like the spackle for the damaged wall. We create strength by noticing strength and allowing the flat spots in our lives to be part of our humanity. Mistakes can build confidence not erode it. Babe Ruth struck out more than anyone. Hope and courage create confidence. A nurturing environment and gentle strong support is the spackle giving us confidence to find our way in the world; confidence to leave our roots and soar.

❖❖❖❖❖❖
Validate and investigate conflict

Conflict is inevitable, the job of parents and care givers is to reduce tension, not escalate it, to learn and teach about conflict, not solve it. Approach conflict with an intent to learn and to validate the feelings and problems the conflict poses without fixing. If the conflict is with us we can own our part and offer alternatives, compromises, apologies or simple affirmation. Investigation should be done without being too pushy. Respect privacy and let the person know we are available to talk more about it.

❖❖❖❖❖❖
Take it seriously, do not panic

Problems often become crises in low functioning families. Over reactiveness by care givers increases anxiety and stress among family members. When parents panic, the fear of children escalates dramatically. Accepting problems of those around us as serious for them even when they may seem trivial to us is a respectful posture. Child problems and fears are often minimized but children do not have the back up of experience. Much of what they encounter is new and mysterious.

❖❖❖❖❖❖
Teach process time

Patience comes from patience modeled. As we allow time for thinking, healing and grieving, forgiving, listening and learning, those around us see and learn about time for their own processes. Time outs, pauses before jumping in or asking questions are helpful for adults and children. "Wait and see" may be an under rated wisdom. Most of the important parts of our life are processes and cannot or will not be hurried. A decision to not decide is a valid option in many circumstances.

❖❖❖❖❖❖
When all else fails, breathe

A family is a collection of people. Components are not the members but the relationship between the members. A family of Mom, Dad and three children has not five but twenty five components. Each individual relationship with themselves and each of the others. These relationships have highs and lows. We cannot control or heal all the trouble spots. Time usually does the best job of that. Our primary responsibility is to maintain our own balance and keep as much sanity as possible during troubling times. Breathing is under rated as a balancing and coping technique. To focus on breathing, breathing evenly or deeply, helps us keep perspective and a touch of detachment when needed. Of course as long as we are breathing, we know things are not as bad as they could be!

❖❖❖❖❖

Tease gently

Teasing is a form of play that can reflect noticing with a spirit of joyful intimacy. It can help us learn to laugh at ourselves and not take idiosyncrasies or life's bumps too seriously. Children enjoy teasing in relationships with strong bonds, it creates an atmosphere of caring funning. This playful form of tension relief can escalate into cruelty and hurts. Resentments and jealousy often come out in the teasing process. Sometimes teasing is used as a sideways confrontation or to get even. Teasing is like tickling, a little bit goes a long ways. Teasing should also be balanced if not equal, with teaser/teasing roles traded easily and often.

❖❖❖❖❖

Say each others' names

Humans more than any other creatures respond to their names. Having someone remember our name that we met briefly gives us a feeling of importance, we were really noticed. Frequently saying the name of those we spend time with is a continuing fueling of noticing and importance. Saying a name can be done in many caring ways and contexts and is something people seldom tire of. Names on birthday cakes, bedroom door signs, notes, books and announcements offer recognition, pride and ownership. Take care *not* to put names on jackets, clothing or backpacks where a young child could be easily solicited by name by a stranger. Pointing out places, famous people and things of the same name is always a bit exciting, like we share in something unique and special. What's in a name? We are.

❖❖❖❖❖
Use terms of endearment

Words are important. What we verbalize not only reflects our thoughts and feelings but also reinforces and creates them. To speak lovingly towards another builds care. Terms of endearment are the contractions and abbreviations of love, sonnets and emotional disclosures. Each term is an affirmation speaking to the special bond. The words may be cute, funny, warm, serious or casual, but they all pretty much say "I care." Nicknames can be terms of endearments. The familiarity and uniqueness of a nickname accepted by the person also reflects a special relationship with that person.

Children will do it when they are ready

W e all have expectations of our children, sometimes tied in with fears and frequently part of the dreams we share with them. Our expectations can cause us to push too hard, creating pressure that holds them back. Roller coasters, their first step, riding a bike, word pronunciation will come, not when the parent is ready, but when the child is. The parent can model, encourage and teach but cannot provide the timing. Fortunately each child is unique and works by their own clock.

Responsibilities are earned, not assigned

A s children grow, the recognition of their development is allowing more responsibility and choices. They earn their way into helping with cooking, yard work and baby sitting. The posture toward responsibility as a shared experience of creating a healthy environment rather than drudgery and chore. This helps create a setting where children become willing and maybe excited to participate in more of the business of family and perhaps even the familybusiness. Having confidence and offering responsibility to some one is affirming. Trusting them affirms their self assurance. Responsibilities are a gradual process of children being involved in the maintenance of house, apartment, yard area. These jobs become an experience of sharing and growing rather than assigning and hassle.

❖❖❖❖❖
Encourage and acknowledge work

Encouragement is inspiring of courage toward a task or goal. We inspire with our own work attitude and pride of accomplishments. We inspire courage by risking and going beyond what is necessary or expected. Teaching children about work begins early as does teaching them about rewards. Noticing the pride and good feelings of a child's block construction, clean dishes, mud pies or weeded garden is the building of the internal reward. External rewards include the earnings, reactions of others, prizes, stars and care that effort can bring. The ability to work and the experience of work is intrinsic to a healthy sense of survival and security, becoming an instinct traveling with us through life. Industry is a stage of child development where tasks are able to be completed with patience and effort. Learning is the chief industry of childhood needs to as well as other work and a healthy attitude towards work must be modeled and supported.

❖❖❖❖❖
Play is the work of children,
we are all children

The stage of development preceding industry is initiative. Children who are supported for and given room to initiate games, ideas, interests, imagination and play are happier and tend to be more creative and industrious throughout life. Children learn to be productive, social and competent through play. A "child like" approach to life is playful and can stay with us as adults. Play is not so much in what we do but in our attitude toward and style of doing it. For some of us our jobs can be a form of play and even when not, we can still be playful on the job. A playful spirit is forever young and fresh, while seasoned with wisdom and experience.

❖❖❖❖❖

Cherish life

We all share in a gift that comes in a variety of shapes, sizes and colors. The gift is life. In learning to cherish our personal life we can sense and enjoy the oneness of all life. We can model guardianship and noticing, enjoying and learning while protecting the more vulnerable packages of life on earth. How we treat ourselves and each other is the core of learning to cherish life. When children are cherished and protected they are able to offer what they have received, the cherishing and protecting of the life is around them.

❖❖❖❖❖

Adopt a pet

Adoption is different than buying or owning. When we include a pet in the family, we give the opportunity to practice the guardianship and share the love. Pets can provide awareness, companionship, nurturing and responsibility. The pet can be a family pet or an individual's, but ownership is not the issue. Pets are not about ownership but are about loanership and guardianship. The pet must be compatible with the setting of the family. The decision to adopt a puppy or a guppy must be based on the interests, needs, settings and community of the family.

❖❖❖❖❖❖

Feed and neuter your pet

Responsibilities in pet ownership include ensuring the survival of the pet. Feeding can be a shared experience or done by one individual but everyone involved with the pet is responsible to be sure the pet is fed. If the person who's turn it is or who's responsibility it is shirks the duty, it is still the responsibility of others to pick up on the duty or to ensure it is done. Depending on the pet and the circumstances, neutering is also a responsibility. The problems un-neutered pets can cause for a family and community have a simple resolution. The miracle of life that children can learn in having pets multiply is indeed a blessing and spectacular, but the question remains of what happens to the additional family members now? Are they going to be destroyed? Is the family going to be resentful of trying to get rid of pets? Do the children attach and create power struggles in keeping more pets than the family can realistically have? The breeding of pets need to be a decision done before hand.

❖❖❖❖❖❖
Demand respect for creation

Respect for creation includes how we are respectful of ourselves, how we treat pets, our consumption, recycling. It is also the noticing and learning about the world around us, understanding and noticing the consequences of our actions. Children can be impulsive and short sighted. When behavior involves the harming of a precious part of our natural world or hurt to a creature, we must demand change. Our planet depends on it.

❖❖❖❖❖❖
Keep rules to a minimum

And that's a rule! The more rules and restrictions we place on others, the more likely they are to react, rebel, and act out. People struggle more when feeling restricted. Our lives are easier with fewer rules because there is less time and effort spent on monitoring and enforcing. Children tend to test limits and break rules. Keep the rules attached to important issues and safety concerns. Do not try to regulate what is already working well. Some things we cannot regulate anyway. Rules about friends, attitudes, grades are often a waste of time. The more rules we have the more we have to worry about how we will respond when the rules are broken. Rules seldom facilitate change, but they may facilitate dishonesty and defiance. Our society has a lot of rules and the job of parenting is to help our family members interpret, understand and follow so they do not suffer consequences society may enforce. Rules are essential for social functioning, and everyone has to learn to play by the rules. It is preferable to have behavior monitored by values, respect, and good sense.

❖❖❖❖❖❖
Expect basic courtesies

Rather than rules, we will feel less stress in our families when basic courtesies are protected. Keeping family members informed of your whereabouts, speaking with respect, calling if plans change, cleaning up our messes, helping other members when they are overwhelmed, offering assistance with transportation, guests or special needs are all basic courtesies. When parents are respectful and courteous in their adult relationships and with their children, the odds are overwhelmingly in favor of the children learning respect and basic courtesies.

❖❖❖❖❖❖
Reach toward, not away

Reaching out, even to our children, is a risk. We never know how or if we will be accepted and it feels awful to be rejected. In reaching toward loved ones it is important to put aside one's fear of rejection or making a mistake. Reaching out is noticed and meaningful even if those we reach out to cannot accept it. Knowing someone is there can be more important than making the connection. Knowledge of support often helps us deal with life's bumps without having to use the support. When our children do reject our reaching out it is seldom about us. It may be a stage or place they are in with themselves or their life. It is important not to over personalize. It is usually hardest to reach out to them when they need it the most. Reach toward children when they need us. When we need something it is generally better to reach toward our adult partners or friends. Our children are not there to meet our needs. In reaching towards, ask permission first. Reach toward without being intrusive.

Notice

Noticing provides big dividends with little effort. Noticing efforts to change, noticing where people are and why they are there helps facilitate positive change. Noticing is the true affirmation. To notice effort and accomplishment helps instill pride and build strengths rather than enmeshment. Notice character, humor, intelligence, sensitivity, uniqueness, endurance, skill, respect. Many of us notice our children and their needs with greater sensitivity than we notice our partner's or our own needs. This over focus on them and neglect of us is a common family problem and places stress on all members. Do intimacy building as well as identity formation. It is important not to notice others to the exclusion of self for we are then modeling self neglect. Frequently a simple noticing of offensive or destructive behaviors is sufficient. Noticing helps build awareness and offers a chance to resolve what may become a power struggle or the need to provide consequences to the child. Noticing creation with a sense of wonder and awe is really a form of prayer and an important element of spirituality.

Touch

The most common physical abuse is touch deprivation. Gentle touch is the true healing for physical hurt. Touch is healing for the one touching and the one touched. A friend was recently in an extended stay at a hospital doing research on heart disease. They were using rabbits for the research and had more rabbits than they could house in any one place. They divided the group of rabbits in two. The rabbits were fed a horrible diet, high fats, sugars and poor balance. Over the course of time, it was noticed that only one of the group of rabbits was developing heart problems. The other group seemed very healthy. Since the feedings were all the same food at the same time they could not figure out what the problem was until they discovered it was two different people feeding the two different groups of rabbits. One person dropped the food off and left and the other, who once raised rabbits would stay to play with and hold them. This group of rabbits did not develop heart problems. The evidence seems to reflect that if you are touched a lot you can eat whatever you want! A hand on the shoulder, a hug, a little tickle, a gentle arm, holding hands and snuggling allow love and security to flow both ways. Touch can be casual, playful or emotional, but should not be hurtful, rough, or punishing. We all need to be touched. As adults we often neglect our own needs. We need to be held, roughhoused, soothed, cuddled, stroked, nurtured. We need sympathetic touch, romantic touch, playful touch. Being "touched" is a great thing.

Mirror

Rather than loving our children because they are a reflection of us, we can guide them by reflecting back what we notice and cherish about them. We can reflect back their growth, strengths and accomplishments. We can also reflect back their bonds, dilemmas and flat spots in a supportive way while guiding them through. In mirroring what we see and hear, they have a chance to view it from another angle or light often clarifing and providing direction. To mirror is also to enter their world and to help understand them while communicating in a style reflecting this understanding in the context of their life and culture.

Guide

Our job is not to control or direct, but to guide and guard. As guides, we become pace setters and use our experience to find the paths that are safe but still hold adventure, that take us to the destination without being totally goal focused. Guide in a way that allows the journey to be enjoyed. As sherpas, we are needed most in the mountain passes, in the tougher portions of life. As trackers we must know the footsteps preceding us and use the experience of others to help us guide our charges. Sometimes we are scouts, trying to see ahead, often we lead, but just as often a good guide will follow. Even though we know most of the trail and the best spots, we need to be open to the new and the needs and suggestions of the unique group we guide.

❖❖❖❖❖

Talking is like checkers, take turns

Talking in a family is like the sound of a river over rocks, waves on a beach, and the wind in trees. It is the natural hum of the dynamic family energy; small talk, big talk, playful talk, serious talk, nonsense and great sense, late night chatter, early morning murmurs, reading, questions, reports, stories, jokes, complaints, words of healing and support as well as pain and loss. Taking turns allows everyone in, some may be glib and some tenuous and reticent. Some loud and some soft like a whisper. Whatever the voice it must have its turn and be listened to and listened for.

"Every song we sing once was never heard,
It started with a single voice, singing a heartfelt word.
How many songs have gone unsung,
How many voices gone unheard.?"

Discuss openly sex, love and other four letter words

Some talk is uncomfortable. Many of us were raised with no talk rules about certain subjects. Learning how to open up these subjects with our children helps us retain our connection with them and their fears, problems, issues and questions. Some discussion can be private, others as a family. Using articles or media events may help open the discussion. Many books are available on sensitive topics for various ages. A willingness to talk about our values and concerns as well as hopes and expectations models and teaches. Giving them a change to discuss sex, physical concerns, money, relationships helps us learn who they are. It also gives them a forum maybe not available in other parts of their culture.

Let the fridge be the family billboard

The best spot for notes information and displays is probably the fridge. Those little magnets are an essential "family making" tool. Refrigerators were designed not just to hold cold, but also the activities, journals, progressions, dates and events of the family. The door and sides can be a showroom for art, a photo album and the best place to publish or at least give prominence to the writings of family or others. Newspaper clippings, cartoons, sayings, prayers, inspirational quotes, advice and certainly special day announcements and memorabilia, hearts on Valentine's Day, old photos on birthdays, parents' prom picture on the child's prom day are a few of the myriad of refrigerator possibilities . If you run out of room, buy a bulletin board!

❖❖❖❖❖
Ask questions

Questioning is a part of the quest. The ability to wonder and ask is the foundation of learning. About the age of three the questions begin to come fast and furious. The hope is the questions will continue though possibly with a little different pace and spread around a bit more. Do not rush in to answer. Take time. Sometimes helping the other find the answer is better than finding it ourselves or answering it for them. Our quests to know ourselves and our families come from our questions. To question family members about their lives, thoughts, wants, reflects interest. Questioning without grilling or pressing can open doors of understanding and intimacy. When we suspect something, the simplest thing is to ask. We may not always get the truth, but what we get will inevitably reflects the truth.

❖❖❖❖❖
Get directions

When lost or confused it is time to turn to other sources. There is no inherent value in getting there by our own means when help is available. We may need directions for our lives, our work, our parenting, our relationships. When traveling, many of us (especially men) seem to have an adverse reaction to the acknowledgment of being lost, or not knowing the way, and a down right allergy to asking for directions! Einstein once said "A genius is not one who has the answers, it is someone who knows where to find the answers." We want our family to seek direction from us when they are lost or confused. We must model seeking the direction of others when we are.

❖❖❖❖❖

Request permission

Asking permission reflects a respect for boundary. When we intrude...to hold or hug, inquire or direct without asking permission we are damaging the identity and the boundary sense of those we intrude on. Asking permission before we use another's property, borrow an article of clothing or present ideas that came from another is the basis of integrity and facilitates the same respect from them to us. What we give we will usually receive back. As parents we often react and neglect to check things out. We talk about our children's personal issues to others without checking with them. We may grab or hug them without knowing it is O.K. first. Permission is a sign of respect. It includes little things like knocking before entering their room. Asking to look at their work, asking before making plans including them. Through this they are able to develop a healthy boundary sense and a recognition of the rights, space, privacy and boundaries of others. They develop a sense of ownership about their bodies, space, property and accomplishments. Choice empowers them, freedom is built upon choices.

❖❖❖❖❖
Say what you need

Many of us have a difficult time asking or even knowing what we need. We have looked for so long toward the needs of others we lose touch with our own. Becoming more inner directed allows better modeling of self care. In learning about what we need from others and for ourselves we build a healthy balance of dependency as individuals and family members. Some of us believe that if you have to ask for what you need it does not count even if given. We believe people should meet our needs without our asking. This approach limits our potential relationships to mind readers and psychics! Often when we need something the most is when it is the most difficult to ask. Our shame or fear of our own vulnerability can be a block to our depending on others. We can acknowledge the risk as we model self care for those we care about. It is also difficult to accept that just because we say what we need does not guarantee we will get it.

❖❖❖❖❖
Let people resolve differences

When family members have disagreements and differences our first impulse is to rush in and rescue and solve. In so doing, we may actually escalate the conflict or erode the conflict resolution skills of others. We also may end up being perceived as having taken sides or be forced to do so. When people are left to their own devices they can usually sort out the differences and feel better about themselves and the relationship in the process. Differences are part of the strength in the system. Intimacy depends on accepting and cherishing the differences, not eliminating them. We may act as guides in the process but it is best only to guide when asked to. We may make known our interest in helping sort out the conflict and difference but crashing in is only necessary if one person is or could be harmed.

❖❖❖❖❖

Apologize and seek forgiveness

When we make a mistake a simple acknowledgment and apology can create an atmosphere of honesty and forgiveness as well as create a setting where risk in encouraged. When we learn mistakes are OK we also learn to take more risks. We may say things out of our anger and impatience causing wounds. Seeking forgiveness may not erase the wound but it helps the healing process. A simple apology may not suffice, to really seek forgiveness may involve making amends. An amend is more about a change than an apology.

❖❖❖❖❖

Share your losses

Grieving is the most important emotional process we can learn. It is a bridge between loss and joyful reconnection. Grieving is what fuels the forward movement of lives. In sharing the loss and grieving with others, the burden of the loss lessened. Each family member carries a part of it with them. The guidance through the stages of grief is a gift from those close to us. Another gift given is the inclusion of our family in our heartbreaks. This is an act of love and trust toward them. Our grieving allows the healing to be a family affair for our losses and theirs. The family feels the loss anyway, and when they are included and told they feel more connected with us and to their awareness and feelings.

❖❖❖❖❖

Use outside resources

As adults our need do not lessen but our ability to find guidance and support may diminish. Our children are not there to meet our needs and resolve our problems. Our spouses and partners often cannot. We must find an outside support network of friends, sponsors, mentors and advisors. We may need to seek professional help. Our willingness to do this is a sign of strength and courage, not weakness. When we are in the position of wanting to help our partners or other family members but know we cannot we can then recommend utilizing outside help. Our willingness and modeling to use it ourselves ensures the permission for others to do so. Rather than simply recommend or arranging outside help, we can join in and invite family participation when receiving support, counsel and guidance.

❖❖❖❖❖
No hitting

itting is probably the least effective means of discipline and limit setting. It has no place in an adult relationship ever, and is a damaging process to children. We do not hit children because of their behavior, we hit them because they irritate us. The irritation being a scratch that enters a wellspring of anger. It seldom has anything to do with the child's behavior. Hitting a child works better than a martini to relieve the frustrations of our lives, of our days, of our work. What does it do to the child? We minimize the impact of violence and hitting on children. Most of us hit because we lack impulse control or are reenacting having been hit. Eighty to ninety percent of physical discipline is in fact physical abuse. Physical abuse sets up an altered tolerance level for violence, a posture of being hard on oneself, patterns of self blame, low self esteem, nasty mood infliction, impatience, agitation responses, shame, depression, difficulty in caring for oneself or noticing ones' pain as well as intergenerational continuation of physical abuse. If you must hit, hit a pillow, no one gets hurt that way. Think of how absurd it is to hit a child to keep that child from hitting their sibling.

❖❖❖❖❖
No fibbing

f honesty were always rewarded, people would likely be honest. Honesty is taught the same way boundaries, self esteem and playfulness are taught. When we are honest with ourselves and our families about our feelings and behavior, our children will become more honest. Often we involve our children in dishonesty by lying about their age in movies or in buying airline tickets. We often do not lie by telling falsehoods, we lie by what we withhold or by how we say what is true. The truth is usually known by our family members, but when the telling of reality does not match one's perception of reality, the dissonance causes our family member not to trust themselves, to feel crazy or act out. *(There are not secrets in families, only denial and dishonesty.)* Exaggerations are a little different than fibbing. They are often part of the entertainment value of story telling. The poetic license of being able to tell a story usually includes some exaggeration. Lies are sometimes told to protect people. Remember that we seek rigorous honesty, not perfection.

❖❖❖❖❖
No fingerpointing

About twenty percent of anything and everything does not work. Things go wrong. In fact, this life is just a test. We repeat, this life is just a test, a practice run. If this were a real life we would have been given more instruction on where to go and what to do! When things go wrong, it is natural to want to blame. Some of us blame ourselves. Others of us tend to point the finger at someone. Neither scenario is helpful. People generally feel badly enough when something goes wrong or they have made a mistake. They do not need us to provide more blame. Usually one person in the family is picked for the blame more than others. They play the scapegoat role. When we make mistakes, we do not need to be scapegoated, we need support and encouragement not blame and shame.

❖❖❖❖❖❖
Find family fitness

A family that plays together stays healthier together. Exercise and movement are the best anti-depressants on the market! It is hard to be down when you are up and moving. Our problem is not over eating, it is under moving. Running, biking, basketball, rollerblading, tennis, walking, hiking, skiing, canoeing, working out, working in, working together all contribute to fitness. Playful movement and physical activity are infectious, the whole family can participate.

❖❖❖❖❖❖
Hang around active families

Networking with other families who are actively involved in sports, play, culture, creativity, building and community give an extended family of healthy role models and resources for support and guidance. Multi-family vacations and adventure can be stimulating and provide new challenges and perspective to activities and relationships. We need to be a part of community, being among others who are active; part of spiritually, physically and emotionally. Remember, active is attrActive!

❖❖❖❖❖
Play outside

Play is the work of children. We are all children. Even a few minutes of play outside revitalizes our spiritual noticing, physical energy and emotional balance. Play catch or kick. Take a walk. Play Frisbee, jump on a trampoline, fish, swim, play tennis or touch football, ski, puppy wrestle, play with the dog, shoot hoops, the possibilities are endless. A powerful insurance policy for playful, healthful, spiritual children is to play with them and model playfulness. Playing outside builds fond memories for everyone. It is the best way to notice creation, to hold the wind, feel the grass, sense the sun, the shade of a tree, the sounds and aromas of nature. The earth is a giant space bound playground, traveling so fast we might as well hang on and enjoy the ride.

❖❖❖❖❖
Jump for joy

Joy is infectious in families. Be silly, make faces and funny noises, do the outrageous and unexpected. Some times the best way to face misery is funning about it. Things are seldom so bad a good laugh cannot help. We keep joy by holding a child like attitude toward the world. Joy and humor flow more easily when we do not take ourselves too seriously. Joy is physically expressed by exuberance and physical play, a light in the eyes, the pleasure of running, dancing and jumping for joy is shared even by adolescence who think it is all very silly. They need so badly to be silly themselves.

❖❖❖❖❖❖
Share gratitude, do not seek it

Many of us give our children everything, but get upset when they expect anything. We offer so much and then look for the gratitude and appreciation. It may not come. Sometimes what we give is what we want for them and what we need, not what fits who they are. Sometimes we cave in to their wants before they have learned to work or wait for the want meaning it is more difficult for them to appreciate. If gratitude is the exchange for our giving we will continually be short changed. Sometimes what we offer is not what is needed. We may be giving them "things," when what is needed is noticing and attention, true giving of ourselves. Time and energy, special efforts are generally more appreciated than articles and things. Gratitude is another one of those "taught through modeling processes." The easiest way to find gratitude in family members is to embrace and share the gratitude for what we have been given, especially the gratitude for our family members.

❖❖❖❖❖❖
Appeal to values

Children, especially adolescents are value oriented. They are working out what they value, the priorities of life. In adolescence the values may seem very rigid and at other times nonexistent. The values are present but not always set in a way that the beliefs and behavior match. Our children's values are usually a projection of ours. When we operate outside of our value system, we model other than what we purport to believe or teach. Our children become more confused and values become muddled. In helping our family members with decisions, direction, through conflict and chaos, by noticing and saying what we see them value, or the kind of person we see them as; gives them a greater chance to follow the path of their values. When children witness violence, dishonesty, affairs, it is very damaging to their value structure. Children will generally reenact or react to our values.

❖❖❖❖❖
Nurture spirit and spirituality

Spirituality is what inspires. It is the inspiration for a spiritual life. Nurture the spirit by protecting from unnecessary hurts, losses and traumas. When they occur we help restore the spirit by providing a safe place to find resolution to the loss or trauma and assist in finding meaning. We can facilitate a spiritual development through our own ongoing spiritual growth. We help our families be spiritual by helping them maintain a sense of meaning in life. Teaching and providing guardianship of them, others, life and our planet, offers a lifestyle that gives life. Encourage creativity so they can co-create with the creator. Continuing the childlike noticing of the world, the posture of prayerful gratitude, while allowing and affirming the unique path of each member. We nurture spirituality when we help them to become the person they were meant to be in the pool of creation.

❖❖❖❖❖
Share stories

Everyone loves a good story. And even not so good stories are better than no story at all and often funnier than the good ones. Stories from imagination teach creativity. Stories from the past teach the rituals of history, myth and tradition enriching the present and steering us into the future. Stories of our childhood tell our families who we are. Stories of our children tell who they are. The stories of literature entertain and broaden horizons. Stories teach lessons, provide moral structure, entertain and tickle. Most of all they are a way of showing love and making connections. Do not just tell stories, listen to stories and notice the story that is around us for it may make a great telling adventure one day.

❖❖❖❖❖
Chronicle and treasure memories

Parents are the family chroniclers. They hold the treasury of our children's past. The past is a treasure not to be lost but to be enjoyed and guarded and then offered back to them. We chronicle the memories by saving the anecdotes, photos, film, memorabilia, writing, and projects. To preserve the past is a gift of loving noticing. A blanket, a bear, a party dress, a chair, report card, a leaf from the yard, valentine, hand print, drawing, a piece of yarn, *(treasures from the past, allow childhood to last.)* The memories are our trust. The past is part of the never ending story of us.

❖❖❖❖❖❖
Value tradition

Some of the things family members complain about the most are the very things they remember with joy or fondness years later. These are the rituals and traditions giving comfort in their consistency and providing the richness and togetherness that is the essence of family. Traditions may include Sunday morning church and breakfast, Friday evening popcorn and rented video, third week of August vacation on the lake. It may be evening sunset watching, family bike rides, Saturday house cleaning, vacation post cards. Any act of togetherness or noticing done with a repetition can become a cherished ritual. A note of caution: overdoing ritual or forcing everyone to participate all the time can alter the experience from joy to resentment. Inviting and making available is the best tradition. Some family processes everyone may be expected to be involved in.

❖❖❖❖❖❖
Go together

There is strength in numbers. When the family travels and is together, the bond of care develops and a sense of safety is built. One of the basic needs we all have is a sense of belonging. Belonging is truly felt when we are in a common place. Children handle the stress of travel much better than the stress of being left repetitively. Couples who do their best in sharing the journey experience the deepening of intimacy and commitment. We all need breaks, but they should be just that, breaks. The norm of the family is the group, interacting, teaching, nurturing and above all, noticing the world side by side.

❖❖❖❖❖

Let the world in

An open door policy with the world provides the integration of reality and wisdom. Our families are safer when they understand the world and have had exposure to it. Multi-cultural experiences enrich and allow more choices. The myths and legends, experiences and awareness of others who enter our world, fuel the richness of our family life and personal creativity. Becoming familiar with the art, literature and history of diverse groups helps develop the sense of guardianship and the spirituality of noticing with wonder the nuances and various hues of all life.

❖❖❖❖❖

Nourish Humor

Humor is what is truly human. It's the flight of our fancy as well as the nose dives of our pride. Humor comes with not taking ourselves too seriously, with noticing the strange and wonderful anomalies of life. Laugh lines are life lines. Humor short cuts shame and builds peace, joy and intimacy. Humor is not necessarily the ability to tell jokes but to enjoy the joke so often built into each part of our existence.

❖❖❖❖❖❖
Enhance hope

Hope is more than a feeling, it is the guiding towards a better place. Hope is the belief in the future, the betterment of life processes that come with time. It instills movement and positive action while dissolving despair and depression. Our hope gives flight to fantasy and creativity. It allows an investment in the present. To take away hope is the crushing of spirit. Things can feel awful but the hopelessness is a temporary symptom of the situation. Hope is a dream, energy moving toward reality. Speak the language of hope, share the dreams of hope, instill the messages of hope in those we love. Plant and nurture the seed of hope in our own heart and the changing seasons will bring the harvest time.

❖❖❖❖❖❖
Deliver dreams

Dreams are the merging of the myths and stories of our past with the vision and hopes of the future. The place of merging is the present reality. From an acceptance of reality with hope our dreams arise supporting us through troubled times. Dreams are the stuff of going beyond, discovering possibilities without the shackles of imposed limitations. Our dreams dwell in the stories and legends of heroics, of going beyond handicaps. They are the kaleidoscope of our joys, the joys not of achieving dreams but of having them. The dream of peace and intimacy are to be cherished and delivered in the sanctuary of family and spread from there throughout the planet as our children spread their wings and soar.

May we embrace that we are all one family,
May we cherish and protect our home the earth.

About the authors:

Marvel Harrison, a native of Canada, is a wilderness enthusi-ast and an avid runner, skier and canoeist who likes to play. She has a Ph.D. in Counseling Psychology, and is an author, therapist and lecturer specializing in a gentle approach to self acceptance. Marvel's spirit and zest for life are easily felt by audiences everywhere. She makes her home on a canyon in the mountains of northern New Mexico.

Terry Kellogg is a parent, athlete, counselor and teacher. For over twenty years he has been helping families with compulsive and addictive behaviors. Besides writing poetry, he is an insightful therapist and an advocate for vulnerable groups and our planet. Terry is an en-tertaining, challenging, inspiring, and much sought af-ter speaker. Terry feels most at home in the Boundary Waters of Minnesota or on the pink sand beaches of Harbour Island, Bahamas.

Marvel and Terry, as program consultants to ANACAPA By The Sea Treatment Center in Port Hueneme, California design and facilitate intensive workshops. They are also directors of the *LifeWorks* and *Life Balance*™ programs at The Mulberry Center in Evansville, Indiana.

For information about workshops, other books, tapes, or greeting cards offered by Marvel or Terry please call **1-800-359-2728 or FAX 1-505-662-4044.**

Kellogg Harrison Family & Relationship Series
Parenting & Healthy Family Life

The Sacred Trust

Parenting & Guardianship of Children and Creating Healthy Families

by: Terry Kellogg, M.A. and
Marvel Elizabeth Harrison, Ph.D.

BRAT Publishing ❖ 369 Montezuma, Ste 203 ❖ Santa Fe, NM 87501
1-800-359-2728

Cover art from *Reflections* by Greg Michaels

Copyright 1994 Marvel E. Harrison
Harrison, Marvel • Kellogg, Terry
ISBN 1-880257-09-2

∎∎∎ *Books offered by BRAT Publishing:*

Broken Toys Broken Dreams *Understanding and Healing Codependency, Compulsive Behaviors and Family* Terry Kellogg

attrACTIVE WOMEN *A Physical Fitness Approach To Emotional & Spiritual Well-Being* Marvel Harrison & Catharine Stewart-Roache

Finding Balance *12 Priorities For Interdependence And Joyful Living* Kellogg Harrison Family & Relationship Series

Pathways to Intimacy *Communicating With Care & Resolving Differences* Kellogg Harrison Family & Relationship Series

The Sacred Trust *The Parenting & Guardianship of Children and Creating Healthy Families* Kellogg Harrison Family & Relationship Series

∎∎∎ *Inspirational & Gift Books offered by BRAT Publishing:*

Butterfly Kisses *Little Intimacies For Sharing!* Harrison & Kellogg & Michaels

Hummingbird Words *Self Affirmations & Notes To Nurture By* Harrison & Kellogg & Michaels

Roots & Wings *Words On Growing A Family* Harrison & Kellogg & Michaels

Reflections *Guideposts and Images For The Journey* Harrison & Kellogg & Michaels

On Eagle's Wings *Words And Images for Your Spirit To Soar* Kellogg & Harrison & Firth

∎∎∎ *Also Available from BRAT Publishing:*

marvel notes™ Elegant & delightful greeting cards

Educational videos and audios on families and relationships

BRAT Publishing, 369 Montezuma, Suite 203, Santa Fe, NM 87501 1-800-359-2728 FAX 1-505-662-4044
Printed in USA